A Dorling Kindersley Book

Text Terry Martin
Project Editor Caroline Bingham
Senior Art Editor Sarah Wright-Smith
Deputy Managing Editor Mary Ling
Production Louise Barratt
Medical Consultant Dr Thomas Kramer
MBBS, MRCS, LRCP
Picture Researcher Lorna Ainger
Additional photography by Paul Bricknell,
Philip Dowell, R.K. Emp, Jo Foord,
Barnabas Kindersley, Dave King,
Ian O'Leary, Susanna Price,
Tim Ridley, Steve Shott.

First published in Great Britain in 1996
by Dorling Kindersley Limited,
) Henrietta Street, London WC2E 8PS

A CIP catalogue record for this book
is available from the British Library.

ISBN: 0-7513-5457-0

Colour reproduction by Chromagraphics, Singapore
Printed and bound in Italy by L.E.G.O.

The publisher would like to thank the following
for their kind permission to reproduce their photographs:
t top, b bottom, l left, r right, c centre FC front cover
The Image Bank: Blue Lemon 20-21c,
Romilly Lockyer endpapers; Tony Stone Images:
Lori Adamski Peek 16-17c, Peter Cade 12-13,
Bruce Forster 11br, Andy Sacks 15br.

Contents

WHY

do we laugh?

Questions children ask about the human body

DK

DORLING KINDERSLEY

London • New York • Stuttgart • Moscow

Why do we laugh?

Laughter is one way of releasing tension when you find something funny. Your face muscles lift up the corners of your lips, and

Why do I cry?
A good long cry is another way to release tension. A tear gland in each eye produces water as soon as your brain says "turn on the tap". Tears also help to wash dust or eyelashes out of your eyes.

your breathing muscle, or diaphragm, pushes air through your voice box.

Why am I ticklish?
Your body has lots of sensitive spots. When they are touched lightly, your brain makes you react quickly, but since it doesn't hurt, you laugh!

Why do

Food is very important and feeling hungry is your body's way of telling you that you need to eat. Food gives your body the energy to work properly and to help you grow.

Why am I thirsty?
Your body contains water, which you lose all the time by sweating and going to the toilet. Feeling thirsty is your brain's way of saying that it's time to replace this lost water.

get hungry?

Why does my tummy rumble?
Growls and gurgles from your tummy
can sound funny. They happen when
your tummy is empty of food and
its muscles are churning
up the gas and
juices left inside.

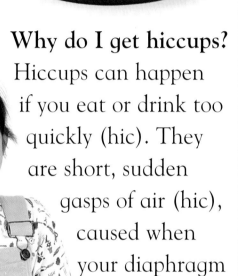

Why do I get hiccups?
Hiccups can happen
if you eat or drink too
quickly (hic). They
are short, sudden
gasps of air (hic),
caused when
your diaphragm
moves up and
down more sharply
than usual.

Why do I lose m

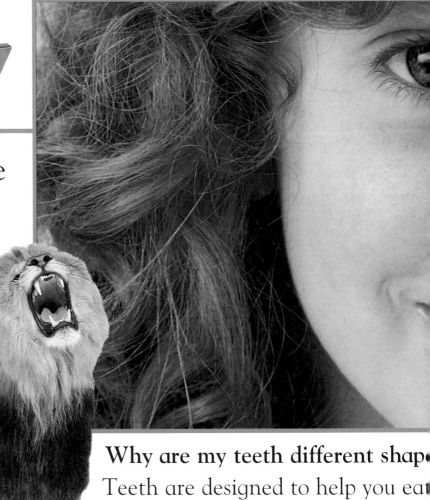

You have to lose your baby, or milk, teeth to make room for an adult set. Children have only 20 teeth. Most grown-ups have 32.

Why are my teeth different shap
Teeth are designed to help you eat
You have biters at the front, sharp
tearers at the sides, and flat chewers

baby teeth?

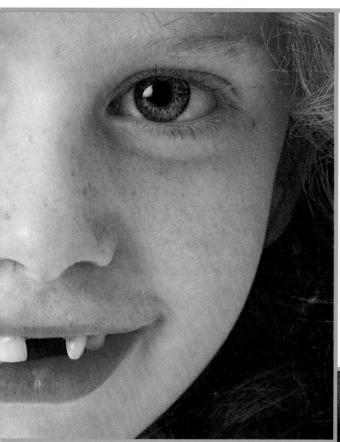

Why do I have to brush my teeth?
Millions of tiny germs live in your mouth, feeding on food stuck between your teeth. Unless you brush well, these germs will make your smile disappear – tooth by tooth.

molars at the back. Animals ow special teeth, too. Lions have ng fangs to tear meat, while cows ve lots of molars to munch grass.

The sun releases harmful ultraviolet rays that can cause your skin to burn – and that hurts! Sunscreen stops these rays from reaching your skin.

Why do I have freckles?
You have a dark brown colouring called melanin in your skin. Freckles appear where there are patches of melanin.

wear sunscreen?

Why do people have different coloured skin?

A person's skin colour depends how much melanin there is in the top layer of the skin, the epidermis. The more melanin, the darker the skin colour. If your skin has a yellow tint, you have a colouring called carotene.

Why do I have eyelashes?

Two hundred eyelashes help to protect each of your eyes. If they are touched – even by a bit of fluff – these super-sensitive hairs "tell" your eyelids to close instantly.

Why doesn't it hurt when my hair is cut?
Healthy hair is nothing more than dead cells. You won't feel any pain when these dead cells are cu though it hurts to pull them out from the living ro

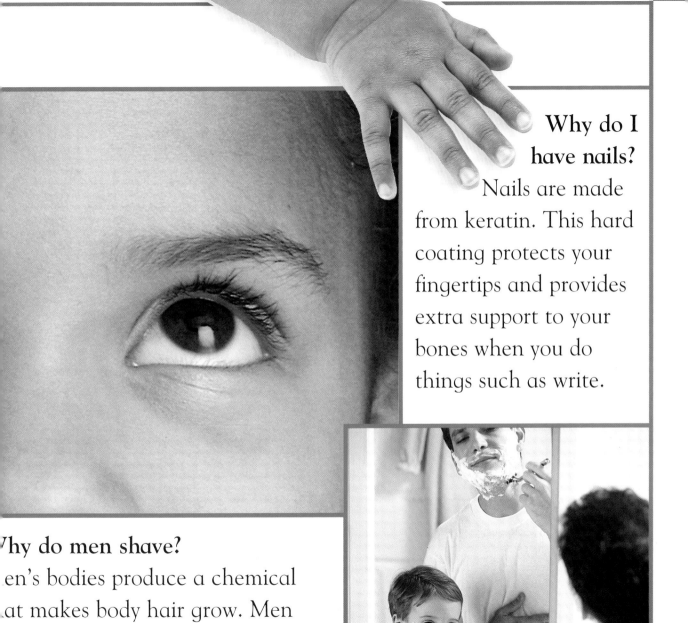

Why do I have nails?

Nails are made from keratin. This hard coating protects your fingertips and provides extra support to your bones when you do things such as write.

Why do men shave?

Men's bodies produce a chemical that makes body hair grow. Men have to stop beards from growing.

Why does my heart bea

"Wait for me!" When you run or exercise your heart beats faster than normal to rush oxygen-rich blood to your hard-working muscles, where it is used to make energy.

Why do I blush?
Just under your skin's surface are tiny blood vessels. When you are embarrassed these vessels widen, so more blood flows through them, making your face red.

...hy do I have veins?

...ur heart pumps blood to every far ...rner of your body. Veins return blood ... the heart for fresh supplies of oxygen.

Why do headstands turn my face red?

You're not meant to walk around on your head, so your heart has a hard time keeping blood away from there if you're the wrong way up.

Why are there twins?

No, you're not seeing double! A baby grows from a fertilized egg. Identical twins are born when this egg splits into two parts.

Why do people have different coloured eyes?

In giving you life, your parents passed on a special mixture of chemicals called genes, which determined the way you look – including your eye colour.

Why is my hair curly?

Human heads are like giant pin-cushions, full of tiny holes, or follicles, from which hairs grow. Round follicles produce straight hair. Curly hairs come from flat follicles.

Why do I have t

Everybody needs a good night's sleep. It's when your brain sorts out the things that happen each day, and sends messages to heal any aches or pains.

Why do babies sleep so much?
Newborn babies will happily sleep for 20 hours a day (with lots of waking up in between!). They need plenty of sleep because they have a lot of growing to do.

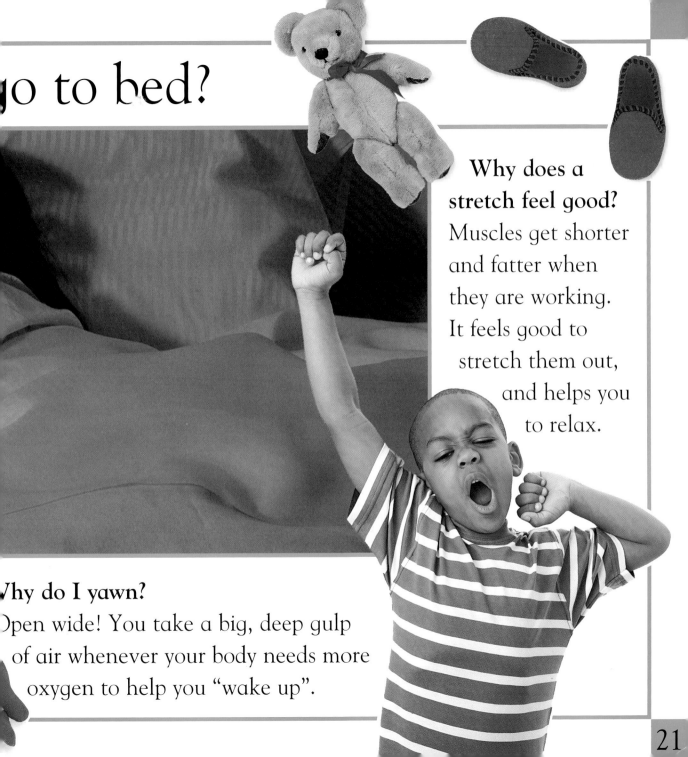

go to bed?

Why does a stretch feel good? Muscles get shorter and fatter when they are working. It feels good to stretch them out, and helps you to relax.

Why do I yawn?

Open wide! You take a big, deep gulp of air whenever your body needs more oxygen to help you "wake up".

21